MW00885876

I WONDER WHO LIVES IN THAT TREE

I WONDER WHO LIVES IN THAT TREE

WRITTEN BY

Scott Bryan

PICTURES BY

Emma Bryan

TEXT COPYRIGHT © 2023 BY SCOTT BRYAN
ILLUSTRATIONS COPYRIGHT © 2023 BY EMMA BRYAN

ALL RIGHTS RESERVED
NO PART OF THIS PUBLICATION MAY BE REPRODUCED IN WHOLE OR IN PART, OR STORED IN A RETRIEVAL SYSTEM, OR
TRANSMITTED IN ANY FORM OR BY ANY MEANS, ELECTRONIC, MECHANICAL, PHOTOCOPYING, RECORDING, OR
OTHERWISE, WITHOUT WRITTEN PERMISSION OF THE COPYRIGHT HOLDER.

ISBN 9798863903194

ILLUSTRATIONS WERE DONE IN WATERCOLOR ON WATERCOLOR PAPER

BRYANBOOKS.NET

DEDICATION

TO ALL OF THOSE CREATURES WHO MAY OR MAY NOT ACTUALLY RESIDE IN THE BASE OF A CERTAIN HOLLOW TREE ON THE NORTHERN SLOPE OF BLOOD MOUNTAIN.

I WONDER WHO LIVES IN THAT TREE.

COULD IT BE A BEAR OR A BUMBLEBEE?

OR HOW ABOUT A LONG BUSHY-TAILED FOX WITH TWO PAIRS OF MATCHING DARK BROWN SOCKS?

IT MIGHT BE A BUNNY WITH A FAMILY TO BOOT.

OR MAYBE IT'S AN ORANGE AND BROWN
SPOTTED NEWT.

COULD IT BE A SHARP-FANGED, LEATHER-WINGED BAT?

OR MAYBE A WOODPECKER WITH A BRIGHT
RED HAT?

PERHAPS IT'S A SPIDER WITH LONG
SPINDLY LEGS.

OR A LIZARD WITH A NEST OF TINY LITTLE EGGS.

WHAT ABOUT A RACCOON WITH A MASK
LIKE A THIEF?

OR A FAT LITTLE CATERPILLAR WRAPPED
UP IN A LEAF?

IT MIGHT BE AN OPOSSUM WITH A WIDE TOOTHY GRIN.

OR MAYBE IT'S A FROG WITH A CROAKING
DOUBLE CHIN.

COULD IT BE AN OWL WITH BIG ROUND
EYES?

OR A LITTLE BITTY ANT SO STRONG FOR
ITS SIZE?

PERHAPS IT'S A MINK WITH LITTLE
WEBBED FEET.

OR MAYBE A SQUIRREL WITH LOTS OF
NUTS TO EAT.

Made in United States
Troutdale, OR
10/27/2024

24176128R00029